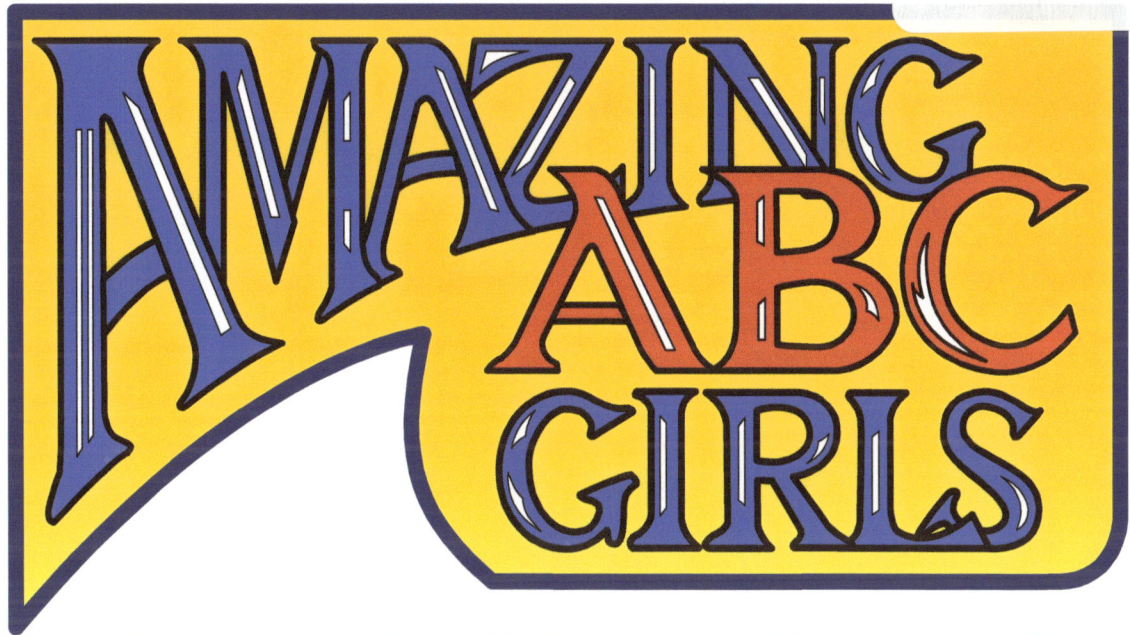

GAME ON!

Alliterative Athletes from Amy to Zelda

Illustrated & Written

by

D. M. Kilian

Amazing ABC Girls Game On!
Alliterative Athletes from Amy to Zelda

First Edition

ISBN-13: 978-0-9994482-0-5
ISBN-10: 0-9994482-0-X

Library of Congress Control Number: 2017915769

Kinematic Press
Redwood City, CA

For sporty girls everywhere

ARCHERY

Amy takes aim on the archery range

Amy is the first athlete in this alliterative assembly of sports. There's nothing aimless about Amy, so her affinity for archery is absolutely no surprise. Archery is all about accuracy, aerodynamics and arm strength. Add an arrow and Amy hits the bullseye. Atta girl Amy!

BASKETBALL

Briana bounds up for a basket

When boisterous basketball beckons, brainy Briana takes a break from the books. She makes a fast break, blazing down the court. Becky's on backup, ready for the rebound. Blair's on the brink of blocking her out, but Briana blasts off and bags two. Brava, Briana!

CREW

Competing crews can't catch Carmen & Co.

Crew is a capital combination of cardio, calluses and comradery. Carmen & crewmates coordinate their cadence, taking care to not capsize or "catch a crab". Completing the crew is coxswain Carol; she is crucial to the crew shell, keeping them on course in the causeway.

Dana keeps cool diving into the pool

Degree of difficulty nor dizzying heights stop daring diver Dana. Whether tuck, twist, straight, or pike, determined Dana dives undaunted. She jumps high and deftly drops into the depths. Dazzling dives do not happen without discipline, though, so Dana dives daily.

Emma endorses sports with horses

Elan and energy are evident every year at the East Beastly Equestrian Festival. Here effete girls on enormous horses elevate over jumps as they execute excellent equitation. Emma and her mare Electra are especially equipped for the exploit, edging out everyone else.

Fencing is Fayza's favorite

Faith and Fayza, friends outside of the fencing hall, become fierce fencing foes with foils in hand. Fencing is a phenomenal way to get fit while having fun. The fearless fencers fly back and forth in a flurry of fancy footwork. Fayza advances, Faith falls back, parry, lunge...touché!

GOLF

Gwen is game for golf

Regardless the weather, Gwen is guaranteed to be golfing. Gauging the fairway, she tees up and hits with gusto. Getting to the green in three, Gwen putts for par. Game over? Gwen grabs her golf cart, gallivanting to the 19th hole for grape juice with the girls.

Hey Hailey, how about hurdles?

It's the first heat of the Hometown Invitational, and competition is running high. Hailey's ahead by a hair, with Helen, Heidi and Hannah in hot pursuit. Hardly a sport for couch potatoes, hurdles builds up hamstrings and a hefty appetite, so have snacks handy!

ICE SKATING

Ice skating intrigues intrepid Isabel

Inquisitive ice skaters Inga and Isabel are always up for an intellectual challenge. Today they investigate inertia, and indeed, it's true. A body in motion, stays in motion, at least until Inga impinges on a snow bank, instantly inciting giggles. It's break time! Cocoa, anyone?

JUDO

Joy & Judy, judo jocks

Joy and Judy enjoy their junkets to the dojo. Whether June or January, the joint is jumping with a jumble of arms and legs. Joy's throw has Judy in jeopardy, but Judy won't be jangled. Just in time, a judicious roll and jaunty jump jet her out of that jam. Job well done, J girls!

KAYAKING

Keiko has a knack for kayaking

Canoeing on creeks? That's kid stuff to Keiko. She prefers the white-knuckle thrill of white-water kayaking. Kinetic energy is key to Keiko's killer ride. Kudos to Keiko for keeping an even keel - and her keister - in the kayak as she careens down the canyon.

Lydia loves her luge for speed

Lydia loathes lollygagging. She likes a sport that's lightening fast. Lots of long workouts off the track keep Lydia lean and limber. Her low profile, leg muscles, and the law of gravity link up, launching Lydia through the labyrinthine loops of the luge track.

MOUNTAIN BIKING

Ming-Mei masters the mountain

Ming-Mei makes mountain biking look easy, but her muscles are working hard. Pumping mightily, she takes in a myriad of amazing views and magical mountain air. Once she bags her peak, she makes the most of a madcap ride down the mountainside.

NORDIC SKIING

Nancy and Nora are Nordic naturals

Nonconformist Nora and Nancy give the nod to Nordic skiing. No-nonsense Nordic brings them closer to the nuances of nature, not to mention they get to nix those noisy alpine chairlifts. The girls know they'll have nifty vistas and rosy noses all the months of winter.

OUTRIGGER CANOEING

Olive opts for outrigger canoeing

Outrageous waves are no obstacle for Olive, Oki, Odette, and Olga. Outrigger canoeing offers an opportunity for oodles of fun. The onus is on our "O" girls to optimize effort and overtake the opposition. Never to be outdone, they out-paddle and outlast all opponents.

POLE VAULTING

Pole vaulting is Paula's pick

Paula prefers pole vaulting; other sports pale by comparison. Paula sprints, plants, and packs a wallop of potential energy into the pole. She pulls up to a perfect peak at the pinnacle, then promptly plops into the pit with aplomb. A personal best for Paula!

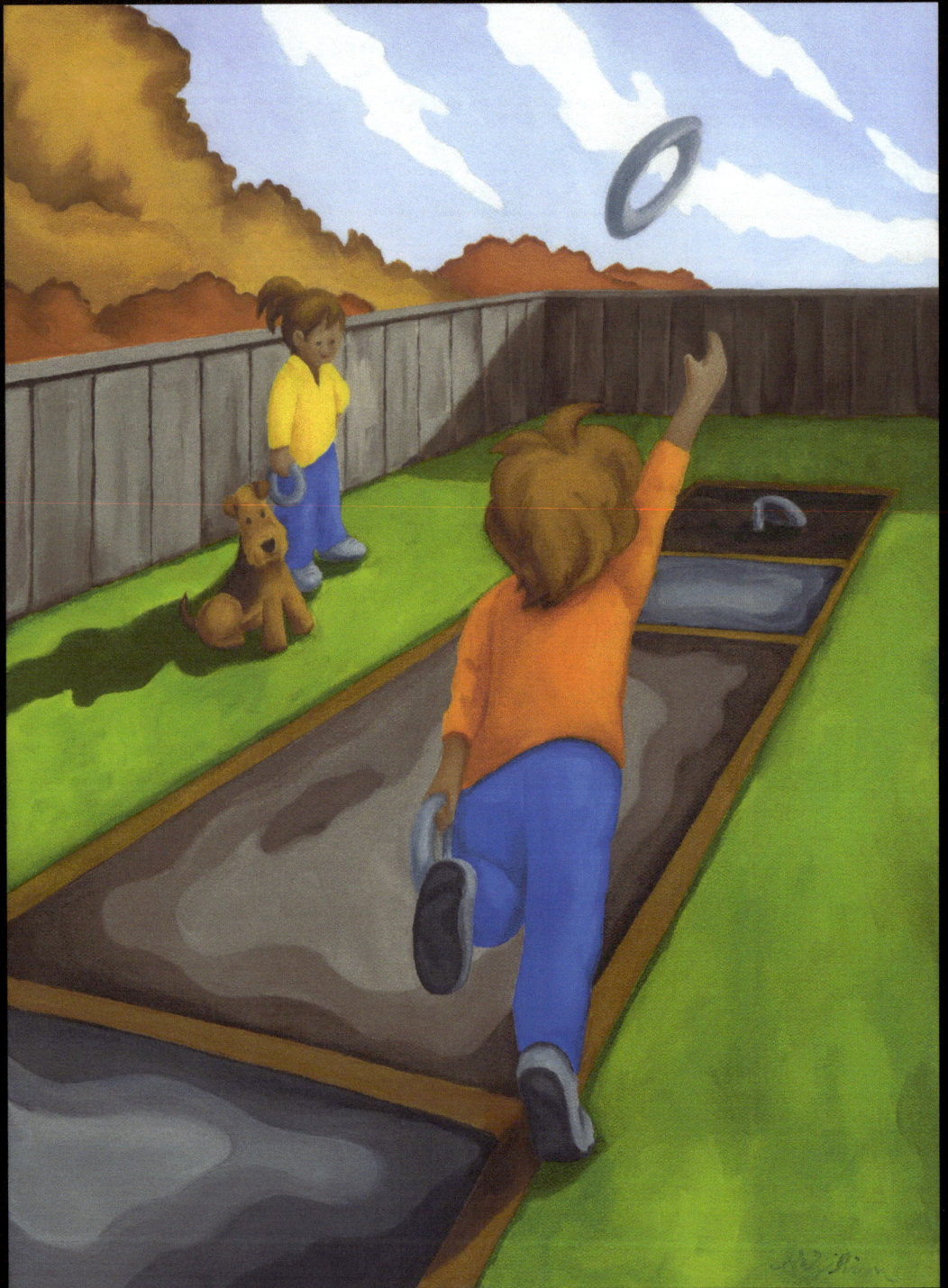

QUOITS

Quickly acquaint yourself with quoits

Queena and Quincy quash questions of quoits qualifying as the Q sport. Played both sides of the equator, quirky quoits requires quite good aim. It's a quintessential way to compete without requiring much equipment. Even their dog Quarks has no qualms with quoits.

ROCK CLIMBING

Rhonda and Rikki, rock climbing renegades

Rhonda and Rikki realize really good routes to the rim can only be reached by rafting the river. Roping up to reduce risk, Rhonda relies on Rikki to belay, roles reverse, and Rhonda reciprocates. After reaching the rim, they return to the raft with a rapid rappel.

SOCCER

Striking Suvi selects soccer.

So many "S" sports, how's a girl to choose? Studying her options, Suvi found skating
too slippery, surfing too salty, squash too serious, and ski jumping just too insane.
She wanted speed, sunshine and stupendous fun, so Suvi chose soccer...soccer's the one!

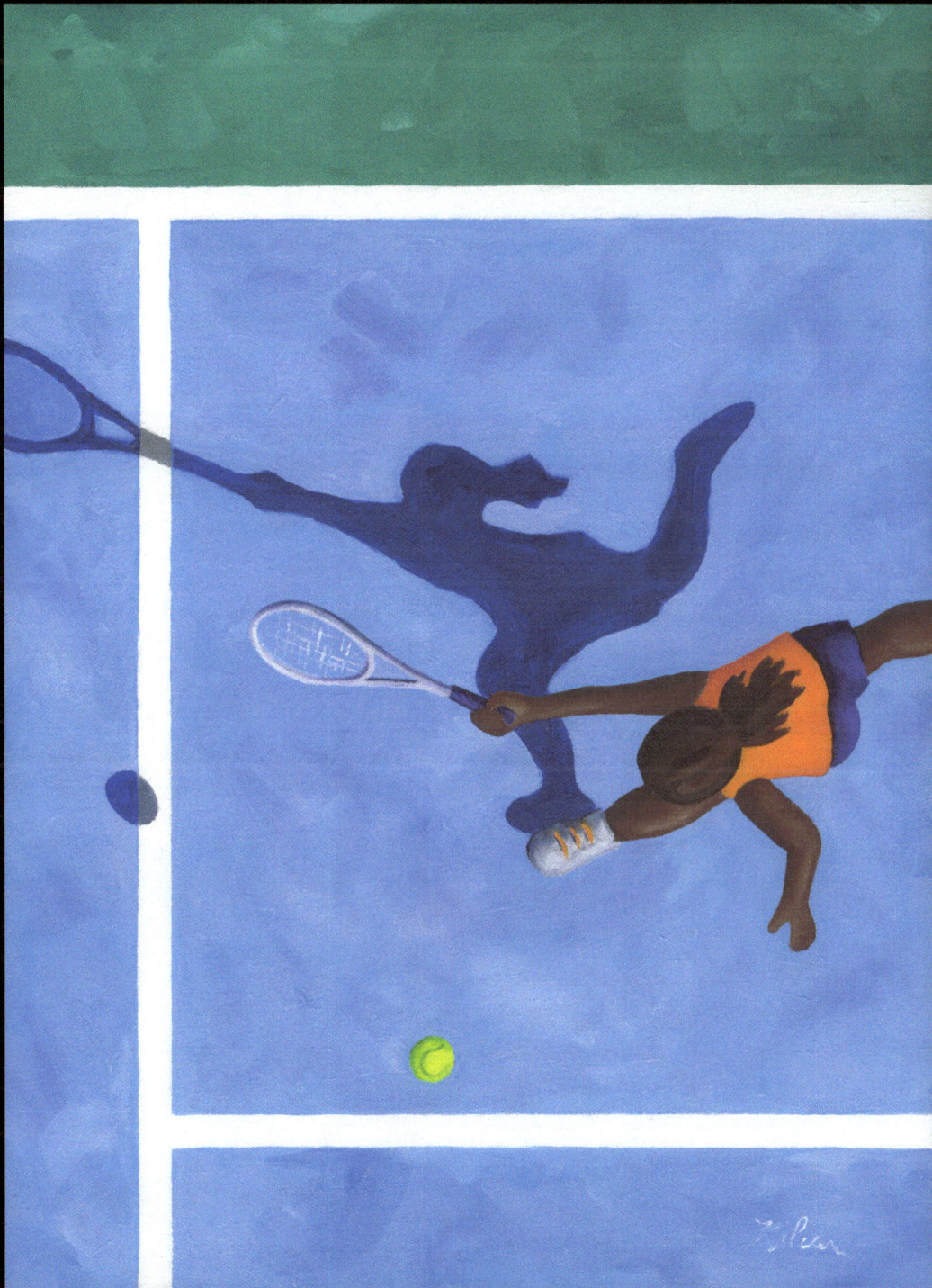

Tanisha triumphs at tennis

Serving first, Tanisha turns a well-timed toss into a terrifying trajectory. A torrent of tough forehands and terrific backhands follow, and she tallies up the points. Her tenacity and tricky topspin thwart all opponents. Talented Tanisha takes home the tournament trophy.

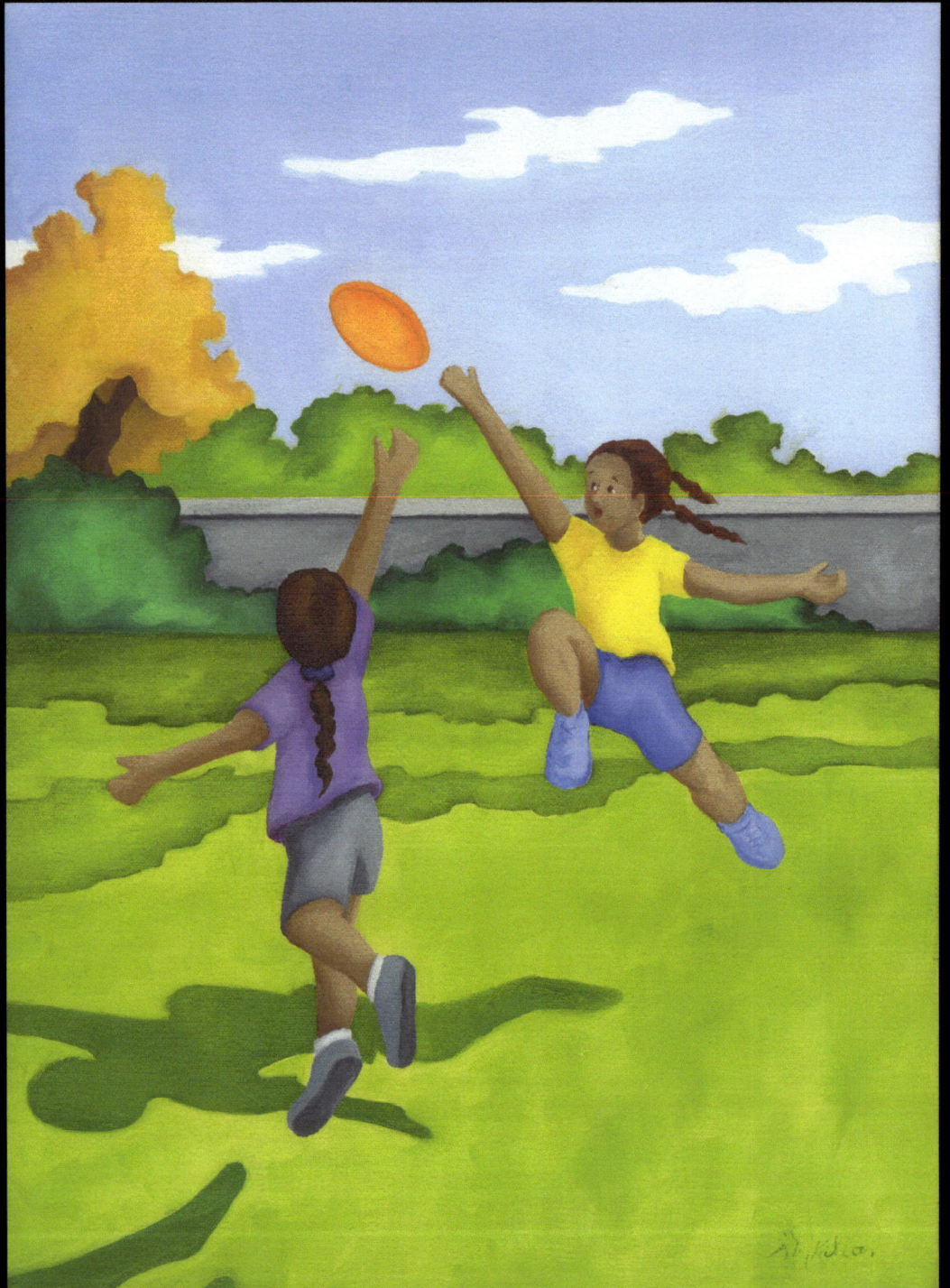

Uma has found the ultimate sport

Ubiquitous on university campuses, ultimate is a game utterly unparalleled for running, jumping, and having the utmost fun. But uh oh! Ursula's urgent leap is undermined by Uma's unstoppable energy. Uma's unrelenting underdogs may usurp a win!

Volleyball is Vicky's favorite

It's a high-voltage game at the volleyball pavilion: the Vista Vagabonds versus the Vale Vikings. Vicious spikes, vigilant blocks and vigorous digs are on view as the teams vie for victory. Though valiant efforts were evident, the Vikings are vanquished by Vicky and the Vagabonds.

WINDSURFING

Wanika windsurfs the waves

Will windy weather cause Wanika's windsurfing will to wane? No way! That's why wetsuits were made. Windsurfing gives Wanika quite a workout and a whale of a good time. With a wonderful sunset off Waikiki, she whips across wicked waves, weaving a whirling wake.

EXTREME SPORTS

Xandra takes it to the eXtreme

With two X chromosomes, it's no wonder Xandra excels at extreme sports. She exudes confidence while executing exotic maneuvers well beyond the X-axis. Skateboarding to superpipe - extreme sports offer Xandra an exhaustive array of excitement.

Yolanda says "yes!" to yoga

Why yoga? For Yolanda, the yipping and yelling of other sports is so yesterday. She yens for the yin-yang of yoga, with its strength and flexibility. Yolanda has yet to meet an asana she doesn't like. But even youthful Yolanda yields to a huge yawn when it's time for shavasana.

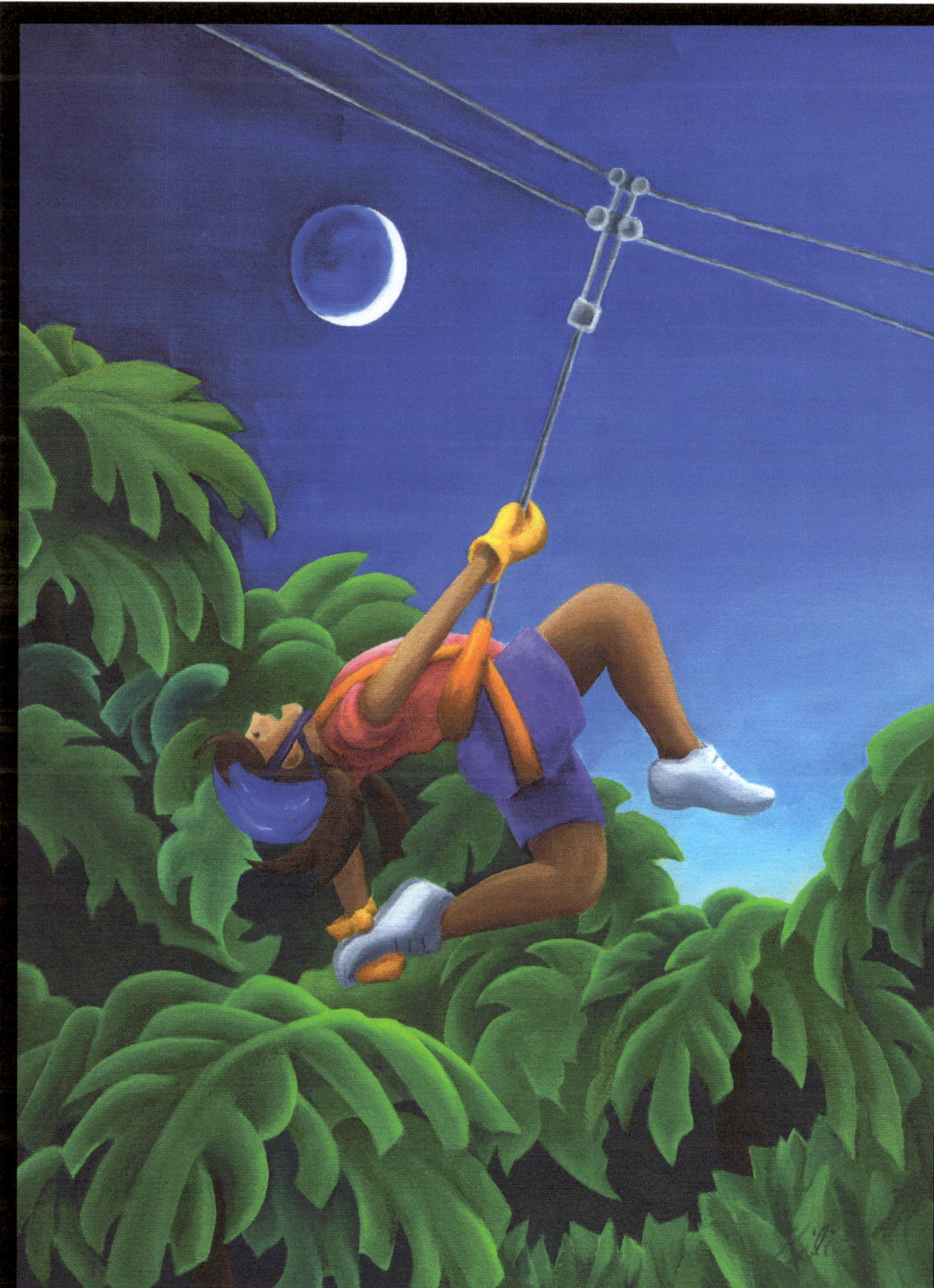

ZIPLINE

Zelda's a zipline zealot

Zelda has zeroed in on an amazing sport. Not just a lazy craze, our Z girl uses ziplining to work abs, arms and legs. Dizzying heights don't faze Zelda; the altitude has her jazzed. Starting at the zipline's zenith, she zooms along, easy as a breeze above the trees.

A  B

C  D

E 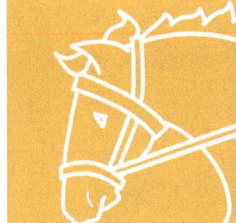 F

G  H 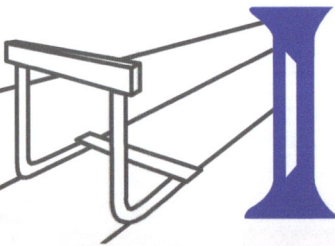 I

J 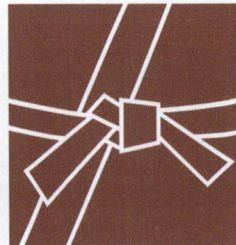 K

L  M

Now grab your gear, get out there...

...and be an Amazing ABC Girl!